My Little Book of
Horses
and Ponies

QED

Quarto is the authority on a wide range of topics.
Quarto educates, entertains and enriches the lives of
our readers—enthusiasts and lovers of hands-on living.
www.quartoknows.com

Publisher: Maxime Boucknooghe
Editorial Director: Victoria Garrard
Art Director: Miranda Snow

A catalogue record for this book is available
from the British Library.

ISBN 978 1 78493 788 1

Printed in China

Words in **bold** are explained in the glossary on page 60.

Contents

4 Introduction

6 Mustang

8 Arabian

10 Appaloosa

12 Chincoteague

14 Criollo

16 Falabella

18 Missouri Fox Trotter

20 Palomino

22 Peruvian Paso

24 Quarter Horse

26 Shire

28 Camargue

30 Caspian

32 Friesian

34 Hanoverian

36 Icelandic

38 Suffolk

40 Lipizzaner

42 Marwari

44 Mérens

46 New Forest

48 Paso Fino

50 The Andalusian

52 Selle Français

54 Welsh Section A/B

56 Welsh Section C/D

58 Akhal-Teke

60 Glossary

62 Index

Introduction

Horses have been by our side for thousands of years. They have carried us into war and helped us to work the land.

« The lovely Arabian is one of the oldest breeds of horse.

Without the horse, we would not have been able to travel across the world – the very first cars were called 'horseless carriages'. We no longer need the horse to travel but we still love to ride horses and ponies.

⌄ **The Andalusian horse is still used to herd cattle in Spain.**

>> **Ponies are smaller than horses, so they are better for children to ride.**

Mustang

The Mustang is America's best-known horse. It was brought over to the Americas by Spanish explorers in the 1500s.

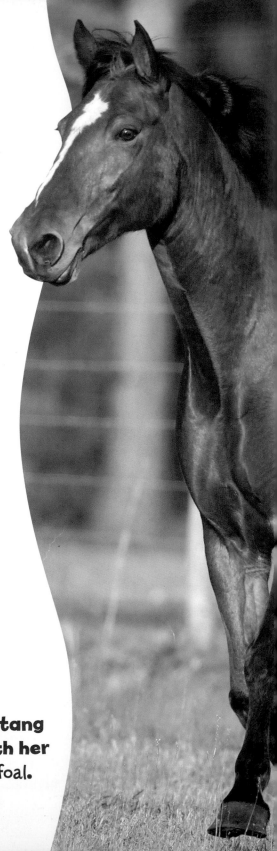

<< **A Mustang** mare **with her pretty** foal.

>> The Mustang can be many different colours.

Mustang horses roam free in grassland areas of the United States. They live in large **herds**.

Arabian

The Arabian is one of the world's oldest breeds and was tamed by travellers in the Arabian deserts.

⌄ The Arabian has large, beautiful eyes and a pretty face.

Today, Arabian horses are used as racehorses and riding horses. They are intelligent horses and learn quickly.

⌃ Arabian horses are found all over the world.

« These horses are known for their speed and stamina. They can gallop for a long time.

Appaloosa

The Native Americans were very proud of their spotted horses.

The Nez Perce tribe lived along the banks of the Palouse River in Idaho and bred the very first Appaloosa horses.

>> The coat pattern on the Appaloosa is known as a 'blanket'.

<< These young Appaloosas already have bold spotted coats.

>> Every Appaloosa horse has its own special skin pattern.

Chincoteague

These rare wild ponies live on Assateague Island off the East Coast of the United States.

⌄ Chincoteague ponies are gentle and calm.

⌄ The ponies are swum from Assateague to the island of Chincoteague every summer.

>> **Chincoteague ponies can be many different colours.**

We do not know exactly how the ponies got to Assateague island, but they may have been shipwrecked there hundreds of years ago.

Criollo

Brought from Spain to Argentina, the very first Criollos had to survive a tough environment. This has resulted in a very hardy breed.

« Criollo horses have short, strong legs.

The Criollo is famous for its strength and stamina and is able to keep moving for long periods.

↟ **The Criollo often has a spotted coat.**

Falabella

Despite its small size, the Falabella is a horse and not a pony.

<< All colours are seen in the Falabella. This one is a very pretty grey.

Just like the Criollo, Falabella ponies are small and very tough. They were taken from Spain to Argentina and had to travel long distances to find food and water.

« **This Falabella foal won't grow much bigger.**

⋀ **Falabella ponies are sweet-natured and make great pets.**

Missouri Fox Trotter

This horse takes its name from the way in which it appears to walk with its front legs and **trot** with its back legs.

>> **This horse became the official state horse of Missouri in 2002.**

Its special fox trot means the Missouri is very smooth to ride and can go faster than a horse with a regular trot.

⌃ As well as being very comfortable to ride, the Missouri Fox Trotter is a beautiful horse.

19

Palomino

With its beautiful glowing coat and white mane and tail, the Palomino is one of the most beautiful of all the horse breeds.

⌃ A palomino's coat varies from pale gold to a copper colour.

∨ **Palominos can be any size and shape.**

These horses can be found all over the world, but the Palomino is only recognized as a breed in the United States.

>> **The Palomino shines like a pure-gold coin.**

Peruvian Paso

The Peruvian Paso is the national horse of Peru. It is similar in many ways to the Paso Fino, but they are two separate breeds.

>> The Peruvian Paso has a long, silky mane and tail.

<< These Peruvian Paso mares look very proud of their lovely foals.

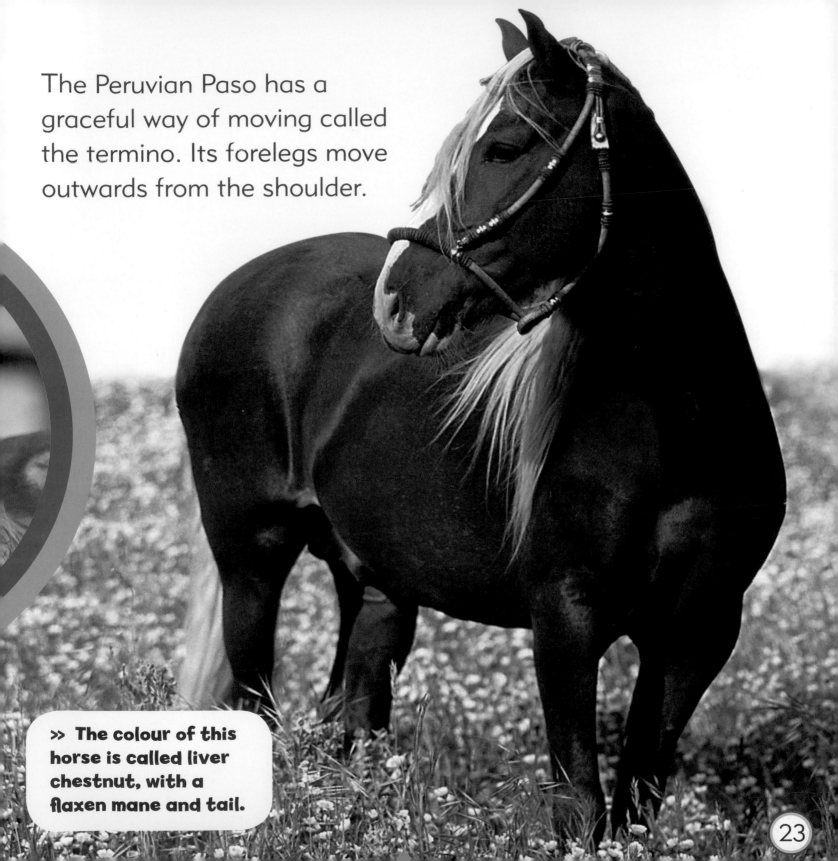

The Peruvian Paso has a graceful way of moving called the termino. Its forelegs move outwards from the shoulder.

>> **The colour of this horse is called liver chestnut, with a flaxen mane and tail.**

Quarter Horse

This speedy breed got its name from its ability to sprint distances of a quarter of a mile. Bets were then placed on who had the fastest horse.

☆ This Quarter Horse's colour is called Strawberry roan.

« Quarter horses often have white markings.

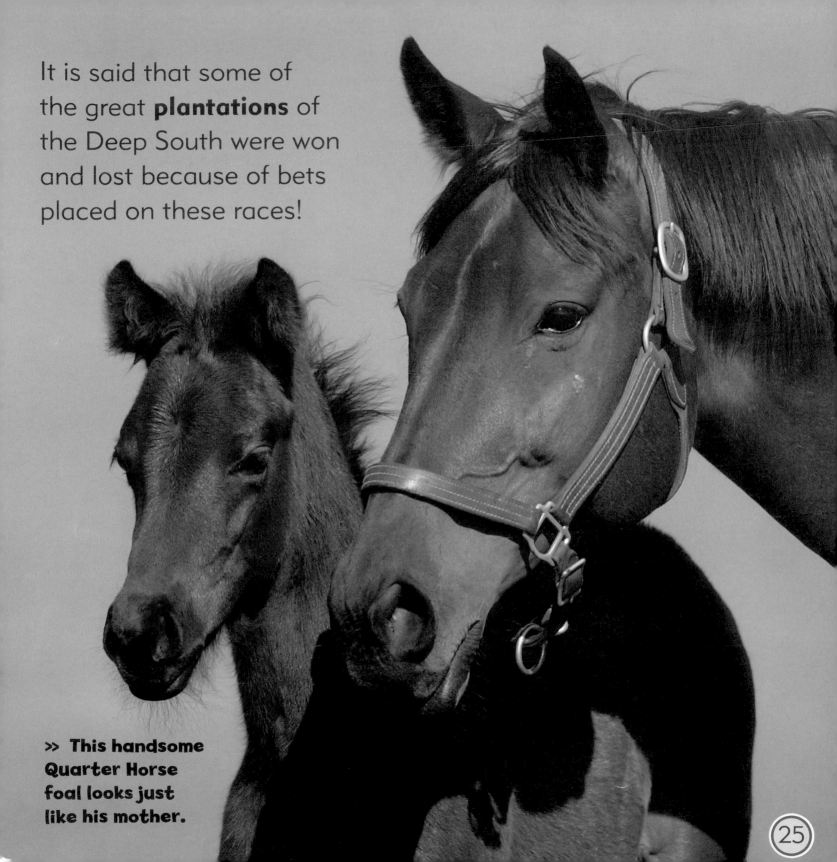

It is said that some of the great **plantations** of the Deep South were won and lost because of bets placed on these races!

>> **This handsome Quarter Horse foal looks just like his mother.**

Shire

One of the biggest horses in the world, the massive Shire is a gentle giant.

⌃ **The Shire is a very friendly horse and enjoys company.**

The Shire was used as a **warhorse**, and King Henry VIII of England was said to be a fan. A Shire named 'Duke' was measured at 19.3 **hands** at the shoulder – that's 1.96 metres!

⌃ **Shire horses were originally used to pull ploughs on farms.**

⌃ **Although the Shire is a big horse, it has long legs and enjoys a** canter!

Camargue

Known as 'the horses of the sea', Camargues wander along the edge of the Rhône River in France.

« The Camargue region is now a national park and nature reserve where the horses roam free.

Camargue horses are always white – or, more correctly, light grey – but are born black or dark brown and lighten with age.

>> The Camargue is thought to be one of the oldest breeds in the world.

<< Camargues live in herds.

Caspian

These tiny horses are usually less than 12 hands tall, so just over 1.2 metres tall.

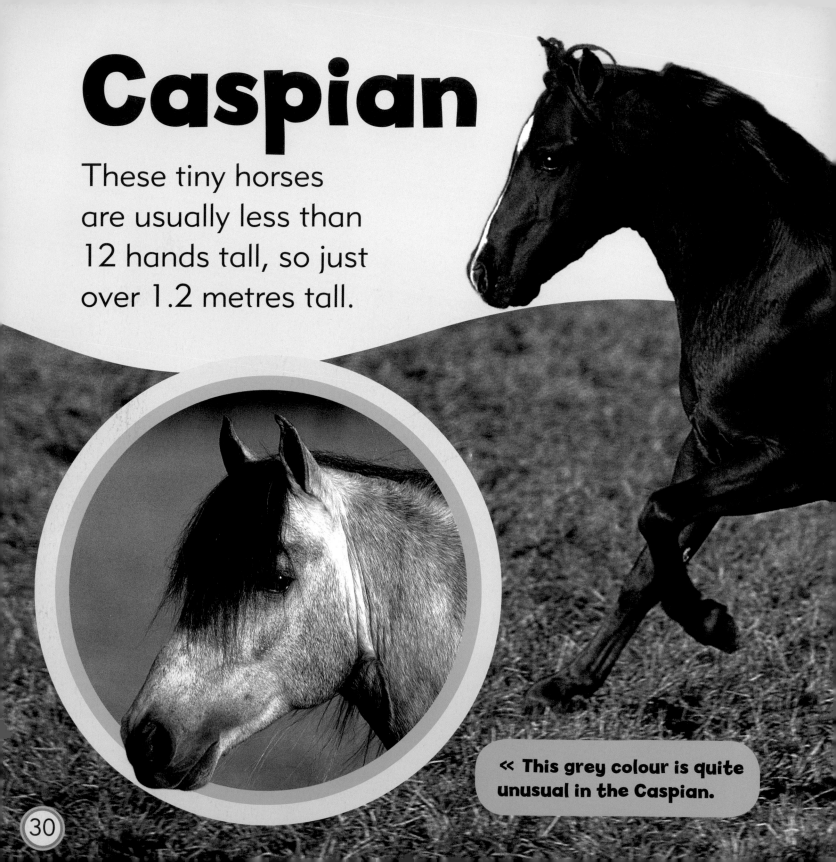

« **This grey colour is quite unusual in the Caspian.**

Although an old breed, Caspian horses were rediscovered in the 1960s. They were found living along the Caspian Sea in Iran.

⌄ **The Caspian has a smooth canter that is comfortable for the rider.**

Friesian

One of the oldest breeds in Europe, the Friesian is originally from the Netherlands. It was used as a warhorse in Roman Britain.

≪ The Friesian is always black in colour.

The Friesian's athletic ability means it is often used for sports such as **dressage**.

<< **Although a sturdy horse, the Friesian is very graceful.**

33

Hanoverian

Germany's magnificent horse is renowned the world over for its beauty and power. It was first bred by George II, the King of England, in 1735.

It was originally used as a **carriage horse** and now competes in almost all horse sports.

« The Hanoverian is very good at dressage.

⌃ The Hanoverian moves like it is floating on air.

Icelandic

The people of Iceland have no word for 'pony', so their sturdy little pony is called a horse.

⌄ Icelandic horses can have many different coat colours.

The Icelandic has a fast-running walk and can sprint, which means it can cover short distances at speeds of up to 48 kilometres per hour.

>> The Icelandic's thick coat and bushy mane keep it warm.

Suffolk

The Suffolk is from the county of Suffolk in England and was bred as a heavy warhorse.

<< Although it is a draft breed, the Suffolk is an elegant horse.

Farmers used this strong horse to plough the heavy clay soil found in Suffolk. They are still used as draft horses today and also in show jumping.

>> The Suffolk is all shades of chestnut, from light gold to deep red.

Lipizzaner

Famously known as the 'dancing white horses' of the Spanish Riding School of Vienna, the Lipizzaner is a beautiful horse.

>> Lipizzaners are born black or brown but almost always turn grey.

<< The Lipizzaner is famous for dressage. This move is called the levade.

The school traditionally keeps one dark-coloured horse along with the grey ones. However, this breed was originally bred for battle and not ballet.

>> The Lipizzaner has a beautiful head with large eyes and small ears.

Marwari

The Marwari is an easy breed to recognize because of its small curled ears.

« Both the mother and her foal have the Marwari's curly ears.

« The Marwari is a gentle and smart breed.

« The Marwari can be many different colours.

It was originally from India, where it was treated as superior to humans – even by the royal family! It was once a warhorse and was known for its homing instinct.

Mérens

Similar to Britain's Dales and Fell ponies, the Mérens is a tough little pony with a coal-black coat.

˅ **As a mountain breed, the Mérens is** agile **and sure-footed.**

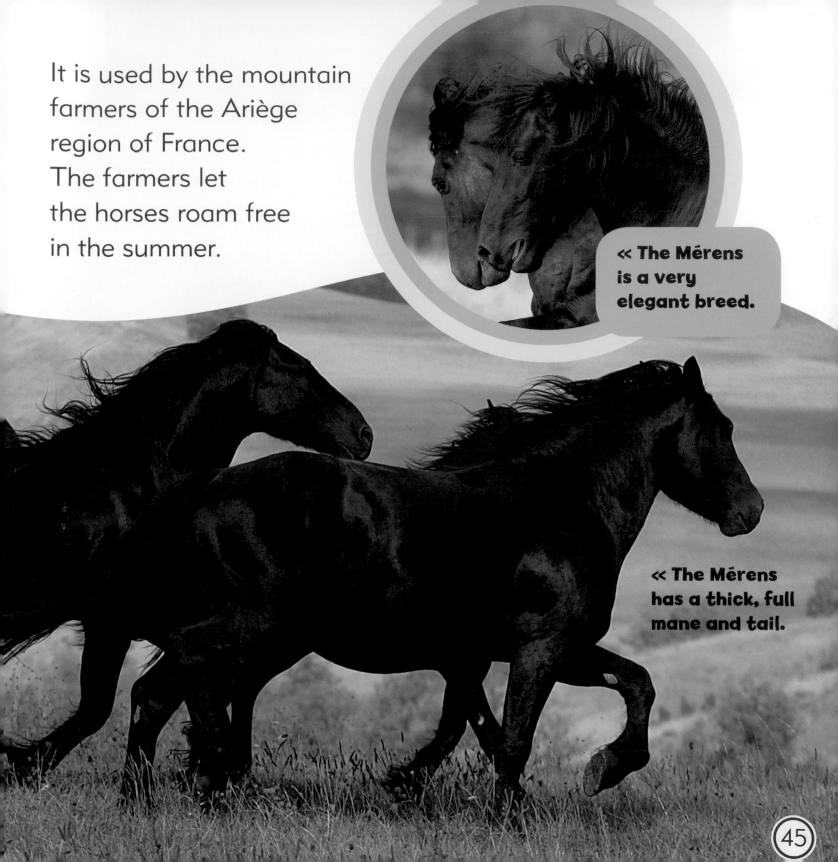

It is used by the mountain farmers of the Ariège region of France. The farmers let the horses roam free in the summer.

« The Mérens is a very elegant breed.

« The Mérens has a thick, full mane and tail.

New Forest

The great forests of England once belonged to the King or Queen and were used as royal hunting grounds.

⌄ **New Forest ponies can be many different colours.**

In 1016, rights to **graze** in the New Forest were granted to 'commoners', and they still hold that right. The ponies are rounded up every year in groups to check on their well-being.

⌃ **The New Forest has a neat, pretty head.**

Paso Fino

Its name means 'fine step' and it is known to be a very smooth horse to ride.

⌃ **The Paso Fino is a proud horse – he knows he is special!**

❯ The Paso Fino is easy to train.

A beautiful horse, it is muscular and compact, with a graceful head and arching neck.

⌃ The Paso Fino has a very elegant head with large eyes.

The Andalusian

The Andalusian is considered to be one of the finest horses – it is both athletic and beautiful.

« The Andalusian's head is fine and set on an arched neck.

« Andalusians are often grey, but this handsome horse is a lovely dark bay.

The Andalusian is at its beautiful best when taking part in festivals back in Andalusia in southern Spain.

Selle Français

The word *selle* means 'saddle' in French, and this handsome horse was bred to be ridden.

<< The Selle Français is a very good show jumper.

The Selle Français is an excellent competition horse. This horse is used for all Olympic events, but is most famous for being a show jumping champion.

« The Selle Français is usually bay or chestnut in colour.

Welsh Section A/B

The Welsh Mountain pony is known as the Welsh Section A. The Section B is a finer pony and is used more for riding.

« **The Welsh Section B makes a fine riding pony.**

✌ Welsh Section A mares and foals.

The Section A has worked hard in the past, having been used to pull chariots and work in coal mines, on ranches and on farms.

✌ Ponies curl up their top lips to smell things.

Welsh Section C/D

The Welsh Pony of Cob Type (Section C) must stand no taller than 13.2 hands. The Welsh Cob (Section D) is much bigger.

« The Welsh Section D is a strong pony, and there is no upper height limit.

The bigger Welsh ponies have a fast trot and are strong enough to carry an adult.

ᐁ **This Welsh Section C has a dappled bay coat.**

Akhal-Teke

With its beautiful, glowing coat, the Akhal-Teke was popular with Roman emperors and many other rulers throughout history.

<< The Akhal-Teke's coat shimmers in the sunlight.

This breed comes from Turkmenistan and was bred by the Teke tribe who lived in the Karakum Desert.

⌃ **The Akhal-Teke is used for racing, riding and show jumping.**

Glossary

agile Able to move quickly and easily

bay A horse that has a reddish brown coat colour with a black mane, tail, ear edges and lower legs

breed A group of animals of a similar type, with clearly defined characteristics

canter A medium pace, so faster than a trot but slower than a gallop

carriage horse A horse used to pull a carriage or a coach

draft A heavy horse breed such as a Shire

dressage A competition in which horses perform special movements depending on signals given by their rider

foal A baby horse. Foal is used to describe young horses under a year old

gallop The fastest pace a horse can run

graze To feed on growing grass or pasture

hand The traditional measurement used for horses and ponies – a hand is 10.16 centimetres

herd A group of animals that remain together

mare An adult female horse

plantation A large farm or estate where crops are grown

stamina Continue doing something for a long while

sturdy Strong and solid

trot A slow running pace

warhorse A horse used in battles during wartime

Index

A

Akhal-Teke 58–9
Andalusian 5, 50–51
Appaloosa 10–11
Arabian 4, 8–9

C

Camargue 28–29
carriage horses 34
Caspian 30–31
Chincoteague 12–13
Criollo 14–15

D

draft horses 26–27, 38–39
dressage 33, 34, 40

F

Falabella 16–17
foals 6, 17, 22, 25, 42, 55
Friesian 32–33

H

Hanoverian 34–5
herding cattle 5
herds 7, 29

I

Icelandic 36–73
intelligence 9

L

Lipizzaner 40–41

M

Marwari 42–43
Mérens 44–45
Missouri Fox Trotter 18–19
Mustang 6–7

N

Native Americans 10
New Forest 46–47

P

Palomino 20–21
Paso Fino 48–49
Peruvian Paso 22–23
ponies 5, 12–13, 36–37,
    44–47, 54–57

Q

Quarter Horse 24–25

R

racehorses 9, 24–25, 59

S

Selle Français 52–53
Shire 26–27
show jumping 39, 52, 53, 59
Spanish Riding School 40–1

speed 9, 24, 37
stamina 9, 15
strawberry roan 24
strength 15, 39, 56, 57
Suffolk 38–39

T

termino 23

W

warhorses 27, 32,
    38, 41, 43
Welsh Section A/B 54–55
Welsh Section C/D 56–57

Picture Credits

Front cover: MICHAEL KRABS,Imag/Imagebroker/FLPA

All other images are courtesy of Bob Langrish images.

In January 2011, Bob was awarded an MBE (Member of the Order of the British Empire) by the Queen for Equestrian Photography and Services to Art, having completely illustrated around 150 books on horses. This award has only ever been given to a handful of photographers and no one specializing in equine photography.

Bob works for equine magazines in more than 20 countries and travels extensively all over the world to obtain the 400,000-plus images in his library of pictures.

Draft Horse
Up to 19 HH
(1.93 metres)
and heavily built

1 hand
(HH)
=
10.16 cm

Horse
Above 14.2 HH
(1.44 metres)

Pony
Up to 14.2 HH
(1.44 metres)

Child
11 HH
(1.12 metres)